LOVE IS A
WILD BIRD

THOUGHTS FOR THE DAY

Eddie Askew

By the same author:
A Silence and a Shouting
Disguises of Love
Many Voices One Voice
No Strange Land
Facing the Storm
Breaking the Rules
Cross Purposes
Slower than Butterflies
Music on the Wind
Edge of Daylight (Memoirs)
Talking with Hedgehogs (book and spoken word cassette)
Unexpected Journeys

Published by
The Leprosy Mission International
80 Windmill Road, Brentford
Middlesex TW8 0QH, United Kingdom

Edited and distributed by TLM Trading Limited (address on page 56)

All Bible quotations from the NEW INTERNATIONAL VERSION,
by permission of the International Bible Society.

First published 2003
© A.D. (Eddie) Askew, OBE
© Paintings and drawings by the author

Editorial and Design by Craft Plus Publishing Ltd.
53 Crown Street, Brentwood, Essex CM14 4BD

Printed and bound in Spain by Bookprint, S.L. - Barcelona
A catalogue record for this book is available from the British Library.
ISBN 0-902731-49-1

Cover picture (printed in full on pp 38-39): High Summer, Olympic Mountains, USA, *Watercolour*
Title page (printed in full on pp 44-45): Chasing the Gulls, *Watercolour*

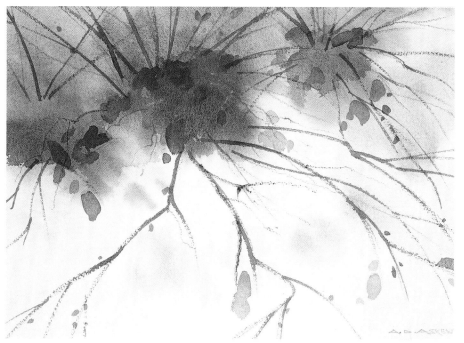

Snow Flowers, *Watercolour*

*L*ove is a Wild Bird. What a beautiful and intriguing title! And how skilfully Eddie interprets the themes of love and freedom in the enchanting story of the robin which opens his latest work.

If, like me, you have been a fan for many years then this new compilation of 'Thoughts' will not disappoint you. It is everything we have come to expect of him – challenging, provocative, entertaining and enlightening.

Unfortunately, as I don't live in Nottingham I have never had the pleasure of hearing Eddie read his Thoughts live on the radio but I could not think of a more uplifting way to start the day. And here you have the next best thing – a treasure trove to dip into whenever you need help coping with the stresses and strains of everyday life. Whether it's a minor upset or a major crisis, Eddie's words are a constant source of comfort and inspiration. And for that I am sure I am not the only one to owe him a deep debt of gratitude.

It's many years since I first became associated with The Leprosy Mission and I am proud to have a continued involvement with such a worthwhile cause. Eddie himself still works tirelessly for the charity. How wonderful to be able not only to bring joy into people's lives with your words but also to contribute in such a positive and practical way to ease the suffering of those less fortunate.

One of Eddie's greatest gifts is the ability to put everything in perspective. His attitude to life is summed up beautifully in his own words: "Tell yourself today that you're valuable, your life is important and that you have something to give. Then go out and give it." And in that giving, show your friends, colleagues and neighbours how God's love is alive today – in every bit of the world we inhabit – and how joyous it is to share in it!

Wendy Craig

Each of these comments was written and broadcast as a Thought for the Day on BBC Radio Nottingham. They are printed as they were spoken, but with a Bible reading and prayer added. They vary in length. Originally the time programmed for them was 1 minute 45 seconds but recently that's been cut to 1 minute 30 seconds. This makes it even more challenging to compete for listeners' attention and to share a positive thought as they get the kids ready for school or struggle through the morning traffic going to work.

My thanks go to Andrew David and Celia Kellett of BBC Radio Nottingham for their constant encouragement, to Noel Jones and all at TLM Trading Limited for their support and hard work in marketing my books, and to Beth Johnson, Denise Halls and all at Craft Plus Publishing Ltd for their understanding, and consistently high standards of editing and design.

A very special thank you to Wendy Craig for her faithful and enthusiastic support of The Leprosy Mission and of my writing.

Blessings on you all.

Eddie Askew
June 2003

Let those who fear the Lord say: "His love endures for ever." In my anguish I cried to the Lord, and he answered by setting me free.

A legend tells that when Jesus was born in the stable he and his mother were cold. Joseph lit a small fire that nearly went out until a robin flew in and fanned the fire with his wings. And that's how he got his red breast.

I met a real robin the other day. He'd flown into the house through an open door and was desperately trying to batter his way out through the window. It was a sash window so I lifted the lower part but that only trapped and frightened him more. So I opened the next window and edged nearer the bird. A wild flurry of wings and feathers and I'd got him safely in my grasp. I carried him quickly to the open window and spread my hands. With a surge of energy he was off, back to freedom.

"Love is a wild bird" sings the heroine in the opera Carmen. Confine it and you lose it. It dies on you. Give it the freedom to fly and, if it returns, it's truly yours. We can offer our love to people but we can't make them love us in return. Caging them won't do it, the only way is to give them freedom. Freedom to be themselves, to develop in their own way. It's a risky business, as any parent knows, one that takes all the courage and the trust we can find. But that's all we can do for anyone we love.

And that's what God offers through Jesus. Freedom. Freedom to be ourselves, to live life to the full. And all he hopes for, in return for his love, is our love.

Lord of sky and earth, help me to fly in freedom and to find my resting place in you.

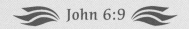

John 6:9

"Here is a boy with five small barley loaves and two small fish, but how far will they go among so many?"

It was early morning. We were staying with friends and I was looking out over the garden from the bedroom window. The sky was clear and sunny. A good day, I thought. Then a sudden movement caught my eye. The telephone wire, stretched across the garden and anchored just below the window, was swaying.

There, just yards away, was a sparrow. He was perched on the wire, tail twitching as he kept his balance. I suppose he only weighed an ounce or so – or maybe I should say a few grams these days – but his coming had set the wire dancing. And when he flew off, as he did when I unthinkingly moved my hand, he set the wire dancing even more.

It was just a momentary thing but it made me realise that even a small event can have a significance far beyond itself. "Oh," we say, confronted by some world problem, "there's nothing I can do about it." And we turn away, feeling helpless. But, if we accept that we can do nothing, that's just what we'll achieve. Nothing. So let's try.

Say something, write to the papers, lobby your MP. Whatever it takes. Who knows, your weight may set the wires dancing. Maybe it won't, but at least you've tried and that has to be worth something. And it's the same with relationships. A friendly gesture, a welcoming word, may make someone else's day. It doesn't take an awful lot of energy to make the world dance – or at least our little part of it.

Lord, teach me to dance in the joy of your presence today.

Overleaf:
Winter Blanket, *Watercolour*

7

A.D.ASKEW

But I trust in your unfailing love; my heart rejoices in your salvation. I will sing to the Lord, for he has been good to me.

I went through the nature reserve the other day. It was cold and the trees seemed to huddle together for warmth. As I walked I heard a snatch of bird song. Then a flicker of movement in a bush grabbed my attention. I stood still and waited. Another movement and a flash of red. Just a robin.

He watched me, head tilted, alert, ready to fly. Slowly, I felt for a piece of bread crust in my pocket. Then, even more slowly, with no sudden movement, I stretched my arm out with the bread in my open hand. And waited. The robin hopped onto a nearer branch and watched. I waited some more. We both, the robin and I, concentrated on the bread. He hopped nearer, just out of reach.

Then he committed himself. With a flurry of feathers he landed on my hand, almost weightless, took the bread and was off again. He didn't wait to say thank you – or did he? I felt privileged. That moment of trust was thanks enough. Trust takes time to build. The confidence to trust someone doesn't happen in a flash. It's an act of faith. In trust we surrender something of ourselves to another person. It can be risky, but it enriches life.

And that was it. Our encounter was over. The robin flew away with his piece of bread. I went away with a smile on my face, my day brightened by a flash of red, a snatch of bird song, and a moment of trust.

Lord, help me to trust today; to take the bread of life your hand holds out to me.

He is like a tree planted by streams of water, which yields its fruit in season and whose leaf does not wither.

Trees have personalities. They're individuals. Tall or bushy, thick or thin, well-established or struggling, they're like people, each with its own character. Sometimes, as I walk around, I look at people and try to work out what sort of tree they are. Just for fun of course.

There are the old oaks. Folk who've gone through all the seasons, seen it all. They're often battle-scarred by life's winds but they're strong, they've survived. Then there are the beech trees. Smooth and elegant people, who grow more graceful the older they get. And what about the Scots pines? A bit dry and sombre, strong characters who take life seriously and with a whiff of self-denial about them. The willows and silver birches? Softer, more gentle, beautiful and feminine – but I won't let my imagination run away too far. Horse chestnuts? Dependable, fertile, generously offering their conkers every year.

Then there are saplings of all sorts. They're the young; adaptable and full of promise. The people who grow saplings used to be called nurserymen – a much more personal word than garden centre, isn't it? And the first psalm in the Bible describes people who live well as 'trees planted by streams of water, healthy and full of life'. It also says they're fruitful. Think about it.

And no, I don't talk to trees. Not yet.

**Lord, strengthen my roots
in the soil of your love.**

Then all the trees of the forest will sing for joy; they will sing before the Lord, for he comes, he comes to judge the earth.

When I leave home and drive through the village onto the road into town, I pass a lovely group of beech trees. They've become old friends. They're tall, mature trees and there's a grace about them that always gets through to me. I love them most in winter when the winds have whipped their leaves away. Then you can see their structure, the trunks and branches that form their character.

Trees are honest. They never try to be other than what they are. Thomas Merton* said that a tree reveals God's glory simply by being a tree. It doesn't pretend to be anything else.

A few days ago I was dismayed. The trees had all been cut down. Maybe they'd become diseased, or were a danger to passers-by, I don't know. All I know is that they've all gone. They're just a pile of logs, a heap of sawdust and a memory. It's sad.

Life moves on. Things happen that we don't understand or welcome. But the trees still speak to me, even though they've gone. They tell me to value today. Enjoy the beauty of the moment. Hold on to today's blessings and don't let them go by unnoticed and unappreciated. They're precious. And tomorrow is in God's hands.

Lord of eternity, my time is in your hands. Teach me to savour every moment.

* American Cistercian monk and writer

...the unfading beauty of a gentle and quiet spirit, which is of great worth in God's sight.

The dog was taking me for a morning walk. It was autumn and a powerful wind was gusting through the trees. Ogden Nash, the American humorist, said that winds are caused by trees waving their branches – there's always another way of looking at things.

At the end of the road are three old oak trees. They'd looked wonderful, covered in autumn gold, but the wind had blown most of their leaves away and was now tidying them up. Piling them in heaps against garden walls. There were deep drifts of colour. Subtle golds and browns. Strong bright yellows, a few rich crimson highlights and, mixed in, some glossy greens from the ivy. The leaves were wonderful to walk through, dry and rustling. It was a whole palette of colour, random, extravagant, uplifting.

The promise of spring had long passed, the richness of deep summer already a memory, but nature was still offering me this great bank of beauty to take into the winter. As though the leaves were saying, "We're going now, but here's something good to remember us by."

And it would be good to think that, as some of us grow older and life begins to slow down, our lives too will offer a natural richness, something of beauty to be savoured and remembered.

Lord, help me to reflect the beauty of your world in my life today.

Overleaf:
Old Pines, *Watercolour*

*...clothe yourselves with compassion, kindness, humility,
gentleness and patience.*

When we came back home from London to live in Nottingham again we found local drivers were pretty courteous. Most of them anyway. You find that hard to believe? Not if you've driven in London. Here in Nottingham, if we're in a side road waiting for a gap in the traffic, within a few seconds someone will slow down and let us in.

I soon began to do the same, but there's a slight problem. When I let someone in, at the next intersection the person I've let in tends to do the same for someone else. And then that driver repeats the process. And I'm three cars down, not one.

Courtesy can be contagious. My good deed for the day – and a pretty small one too – encourages others to do the same. And although it's not earth-shattering and won't change the world by next Thursday, it does make a difference.

I must add a footnote though. As I was driving along thinking about this, an elderly gentleman in a flat cap and a small Fiat drove out in front of me, slowly and deliberately, without any warning or signal. I only just avoided driving up his exhaust pipe. And he never knew. Life can be irritating.

Lord, give me patience. We're not all perfect yet. Not even me.

Every valley shall be filled in,
every mountain and hill made low.
The crooked roads shall become straight,
the rough ways smooth.
And all mankind will see God's salvation.

When Barbara and I are on a long car journey and the traffic is slow we sometimes remember journeys we made when the children were small. They'd read for a bit, then if we were lucky they'd nod off to sleep. But when they woke there'd be the dreaded questions. "Mum, are we nearly there yet?" " How long will it be, Dad?" Time matters and, as life gets busier and faster, it seems to get ever more important.

When we start a journey we usually ask, "When do we arrive?" And if we're on the train these days the answer may well be, "Who knows?" Life might be a bit richer and more interesting if, instead of asking how long the journey takes, we ask what we can see on the way. Real travellers, explorers, often say that the thrill and satisfaction lies in the journey itself. Not in the arrival. The experience gained as we travel is the most valuable thing. If we concentrate too hard on the end result, we may lose the joy of the journey.

Time's for people, not the other way round, and the real joy of the journey we make through life is the people we travel with and the shared experience. Travel well today.

Lord of the journey, give me the joy of knowing you are with me every step I take.

Do not forget to entertain strangers, for by so doing some people
have entertained angels without knowing it.

Georgia is one of our granddaughters. Five years old. The family was in the car and was playing 'I Spy'. It was Georgia's turn. She said, "I spy with my little eye something beginning with c." Everyone looked around. "Car," shouted one. "Cushion." "Carpet." "Clutch." It was none of those.

Finally everyone gave up. "Crisps," said Georgia triumphantly.
"We can't see crisps," someone said. "You're only supposed to choose things you can see."
"I can see them," Georgia answered.
"Where?"
"In my mind."
"We can't see them there," said the others.
"Well you could if you tried," said Georgia, emphatically. End of discussion.

Imagination is one of God's greatest gifts. I'm not talking about thinking up a convincing reason for being late for work, but the gift of seeing things in a way others don't. The ability to put ourselves into other people's lives.

If we could use our imagination a bit more, and feel what it must be like to be forced from home by fear or violence, or because there just isn't enough food for the family then we might be a fraction more welcoming and a little less critical of the strangers in our midst.

Lord, let me see the world through your eyes, and keep me
sensitive to others' needs.

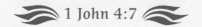

1 John 4:7

Dear friends, let us love one another, for love comes from God.
Everyone who loves has been born of God and knows God.

I was driving down University Boulevard in Nottingham in the slow lane. Actually there wasn't a fast lane. It was rush hour, which meant that everything was going very slowly. A strange use of language isn't it? Anyway, my lane was slower than the other.

There was a milk float in front of me, speeding along at about five miles an hour. In a good moment the driver accelerated recklessly to about ten, the milk bottles rattling excitedly in their crates. But not for long. Soon we were back to the crawl. Then I noticed the name on the back of the float, 'Express Dairy'. My dictionary defines express as 'operating at high speed'. Not much express about that float. Or me, stuck behind it.

Words can mean different things at different times. Take the word love. It's used to mean anything from a one-night-stand to a lifetime of commitment. One definition I like is 'desiring another's good'. Going into a relationship not for what we can get out of it but for what we can put into it. Giving more than receiving. The great thing is that in some mysterious way the more we do put in, the more we get out of it anyway.

So instead of rushing around today trying to clear other people out of our way, maybe spending a little time in the slow lane with someone we love will pay dividends in the end.

One more thing – my dictionary says there's another meaning for express – we express ourselves by 'putting something into words'. So if you love someone, say it.

Lord, slow me down and give me time for those I love.

Overleaf:
Sunlight on the Abbey, Tewkesbury, *Watercolour*

"I have come that they may have life, and have it to the full."

The other day I found Jesus in a junk box.

It happened at an antique fair. Under one dealer's table there was a cardboard box full of odds and ends. It was labelled 'Anything here £3.' I looked through it. Most of it was junk. There were odd plates from old teasets, bits of brass, cheap prints in battered frames, and a few damp-stained copies of old novels.

And among them all, Jesus. A silvery image of him anyway, nailed to a cheap black wooden cross. A crucifix. I picked it up. For a moment I thought of buying it to rescue him from among all the junk in the cardboard box. I could take him home and put him somewhere more suitable, more respectable. Maybe on the wall in my studio.

Then something told me he wouldn't want to be rescued. He'd rather be there, where he was, in the junk box among the least-valued, the throw-away pieces from a throw-away society. Jesus always had time for throwaways, the down-and-outs and the undervalued.

So I quietly put him back in the box and, as I did so, he seemed to nod and smile. Or was that just my imagination?

Lord of old and new, open my eyes to your presence in everyone I see today.

 Mark 14:37

Then he returned to his disciples and found them sleeping.

I was on a long haul flight to Singapore. Among the papers in the pocket of the seat in front of me was a bit of coloured card. On it, in large bright letters, it said, 'Do Not Disturb'.

When you want to sleep you put your seat into its recline position, sometimes to the annoyance of the person sitting behind, display the notice and close your eyes. It's supposed to prevent interruptions. It doesn't always work, particularly if you're in an aisle seat and someone wants to get past you to go to the loo.

I thought it would be great if I could carry the notice around all the time, wherever I was. 'Do Not Disturb.' Bad news? Problems in the Middle East? Someone needing my help? 'Do Not Disturb.' Just let me roll over and sleep. But it wouldn't work and I don't believe it should.

We need to be disturbed at times, to be jolted out of our comfortable ruts – by injustice, by suffering – and we have no inborn right to an easy life. And if we're disturbed enough by what goes on around us, we might just start doing something to help.

One last thing. If we did manage to sleep through the problems, we might miss the joys of life as well. I wouldn't want to do that. Would you?

Lord, life with you can be uncomfortable. Keep me awake, the excitement makes it all worthwhile.

And what does the Lord require of you? To act justly and to love mercy and to walk humbly with your God.

A news item on the radio grabbed my attention. "Chocolate," it said, "is good for you." Wow!

Later I followed it up on the Internet. Who wouldn't, hearing those words? And it seemed to be true. Chocolate, I'm told, contains chemicals that may help prevent cancer and heart disease. But before we all rush out and form a queue outside the local corner shop, let's look at the small print.

The research was financed by a well-known chocolate-making company, and there were only 40 people in the test. You also need to eat an awful lot of chocolate before it has any real effect and that amount of sugar might not be good for you anyway. It also claimed that eating chocolate in moderation – now that's a contradiction in terms – can help us live longer. I wonder.

Today, it might help if the people in the Third World who grow the cocoa beans were paid enough to give them a healthy lifestyle. So, when you hear reports like these, I suggest you do as the Bible says, and be wise as serpents and harmless as doves. Thank the Lord for chocolate and leave it at that.

Although, if they need people for more research on the benefits of chocolate, count me in.

Lord, my blessings come from you. Remind me that they taste better when they're shared.

 Luke 10:33

"But a Samaritan, as he travelled, came where the man was; and when he saw him, he took pity on him."

A beautiful princess was walking through the palace garden with her sister when they saw a frog. The frog spoke. "I'm not really a frog," he said. "I've been bewitched and if you'll pick me up and kiss me I'll turn back into a handsome prince. We'll fall in love and live happily ever after." The princess picked up the frog, looked at him and then put him in her handbag. "Why don't you kiss him?" asked her sister. "Oh," said the princess. "There's a handsome prince on every street corner but with a talking frog I can make a fortune."

Love or money. Compassion or market forces? Which do we value most? A report on TV told of a couple who were running a successful business but they were giving all their profits away to help other people. One of them said, "We believe you become a millionaire when you've given a million pounds away not when you've got a million in the bank." I think that's great.

Of course most of us would like the chance of choosing what to do with our first million, but the principle's good. What do we do with what we've got, whether it's money in the bank or our talents and abilities? We can use what we have for ourselves or we can use it to give something to the community we live in. It's great to hear of people who put others first in such a positive and practical way as that business couple.

Really successful living can be counted by the folk we've helped along the way rather than by what we've squirreled away for ourselves.

Lord, giver of life and love, may I share as much in giving as in getting.

Overleaf:
Winter Hedgerow, *Watercolour*

A. D. ASKEW

By faith Abraham, when called to go to a place he would later receive as his inheritance, obeyed and went, even though he did not know where he was going.

Grey squirrels look very attractive bouncing around the garden, but they lost their popularity with me when one of them chewed its way into our loft. It caused several hundred pounds worth of damage biting through electric cables. The house insurance didn't cover it – squirrels are classed as vermin. Read the small print.

But yesterday I watched one squirrel in the garden. He was on the flat roof of a garage just the other side of our hawthorn hedge. He was a bit agitated, running one way, then another. Suddenly he took a massive leap, out and up, to the branch of a tree that must have been ten feet away. An enormous jump for such a small animal. He made it – just. Then with a twitch of his bushy tail he was away into new territory.

I don't know why he jumped. Maybe he'd been scared by something I couldn't see. Perhaps he saw an opportunity ahead of him. Whatever it was he had the courage to take a leap of faith. To move on from where he was. A leap into the unknown, into the future.

When we're faced with problems we all have to make decisions. Even not making a decision is a decision in itself, if you see what I mean, and it's not always easy. But we all have to move on. When circumstances change or new opportunities arrive we need to do something. It can take courage. We can't be sure how things will turn out, but we need to take a deep breath and jump. Fortunately God's always around waiting to help.

Lord of the future,
hold out your hands
and catch me
when I jump.

Blessed is the man who finds wisdom, the man who gains understanding, for she is more profitable than silver and yields better returns than gold.

I made a startling discovery the other day. It may not change the world but it's this: snails don't have a reverse gear. I went to the greenhouse to water my tomato plants. The watering can was heavy, full of water, but when I picked it up and tilted it, only a trickle of water came through. I put the can down, unscrewed the spout and held it up to the light. It was almost totally blocked by something dark. I poked a cane down through the narrow end and out dropped a snail. A dead snail.

Attracted by the damp it must have crawled in and up the spout. Unfortunately watering can spouts taper and get smaller nearer the outlet. The snail went in as far as it could go, then got jammed. And that was that. There was no room to turn and the snail had no reverse gear.

It made me think. Never put yourself into a situation you can't back out of. Bad grammar, but you see what I mean. People argue and, in the heat of the moment, make statements they can't justify, and then find they can't back away. Too embarrassing. They get aggressive, which makes things worse, and before you know it World War Three's broken out. Or nearly so.

Take time to listen to what the other person's saying. Put yourself in their place and don't push too hard or you may get stuck without any chance of backing away. Leave room for understanding and keep the channels of communication unblocked. Remember the snail.

Lord, it may be asking a lot of you, but help me to think before I speak, and then not to say too much.

 **James 1:19-20**

Everyone should be quick to listen, slow to speak and slow to become angry, for man's anger does not bring about the righteous life that God desires.

A newspaper said a vicar and a pub landlord had swapped places for a day. No, it's not a joke, it really happened. The vicar spent an evening behind the bar and the pub landlord took over the pulpit in the local church and preached the sermon.

I'd love to know what he preached about, but that wasn't reported. Then I wonder how the vicar dealt with any drunks, or anyone who tried to pull the barmaid while he was pulling pints.

But there's a good point to it all. The vicar and the landlord were getting in touch with areas of life they weren't usually part of. The vicar listening to bar room philosophy, the landlord opening himself up to the reality of faith. It's always good to try to understand the other person's point of view and to experience – or at least imagine – what it's like living the other person's life. And I hope their respective audiences set aside their prejudices.

I also have a feeling that, if Jesus were here in the flesh, it might well be the pub he went to first.

Lord of all life, open my ears and eyes to truth, wherever you have put it.

*"For there is nothing hidden that will not be disclosed,
and nothing concealed that will not be known or brought
out into the open."*

There was a report in the newspaper recently about a woman and her pet dog. Every time she stroked it she felt there was something strange about its stomach. Then she heard a noise when she touched it – not the usual puppy sounds – something different, a sort of scrunching noise. She took the dog to the vet. He too was puzzled. He anaesthetised the dog and took X-rays. All was revealed.

In the dog's stomach were 32 pebbles which he'd picked up and eaten. No one knows why – except the dog, and he's not telling – but it could give a new meaning to the phrase 'being stoned'.

Seriously, you never know what's going on beneath the surface, do you? Whether it's animal or human there's a lot more to us than meets the eye. On the surface everything may look alright. "No problem," we say, but people often cover up their anxieties, pretend they're OK when really they're crying out for help. That doesn't give us the right to probe around in other people's lives but it may make us a little slower to criticise and judge. And it may suggest that we should spread our friendship around more. Include more people in it.

A bit more sympathy with other folk's behaviour will make the day a little better. And incidentally, the puppy made a full recovery.

*Lord, when I think I have the answer, maybe I'm asking
the wrong question. Lend me a little of your understanding
as I live today.*

Overleaf:
Autumn in the Lake District, *Watercolour*

The wolf will live with the lamb, the leopard will lie down with the goat...and the lion will eat straw like the ox.

I wonder if you saw a press report about a lioness who adopted an orphaned oryx – a small antelope – and mothered it. The paper had a picture of the two of them together, lioness and antelope, walking through the scrub in Kenya.

Usually, in the lion's economy, antelopes are viewed as breakfast, not members of the family, but here were the two of them living together. An unlikely pair but an encouraging picture.

There's a bit in the Bible about wolves living with lambs, and lions eating straw – it's a dream of what the ideal world would be like. Translated into human terms, it's a vision of people renouncing violence, turning our swords into ploughs, and trying to solve our problems peacefully. Looking at today's world, we're a long way from that, but we have to dream. We need to hold on to a vision of what could be, if only we tried harder.

And it is hard. The story of the lioness and the antelope had its downside. Apparently one day another lion came along – a male, it would be, wouldn't it? – who didn't have quite the same feelings for the antelope. He ate it.

But would you believe it, the lioness did the same thing again. She found and befriended another orphaned antelope. There are always setbacks in life, whether it's Belfast or Jerusalem. But we go on hoping and praying; that's what makes us human. Let's keep doing it.

Lord of my dreams, I look to you today and everyday. Open my heart to hope, and let me share my life with you.

Jeremiah 18:3-4

So I went down to the potter's house, and I saw him working at the wheel. But the pot he was shaping from the clay was marred in his hands; so the potter formed it into another pot, shaping it as seemed best to him.

Sitting on the table in front of me is a present – a beautifully engraved silver bowl. A lovely gift. Some time ago I was in India, visiting a hospital where I'd been invited to share in the opening of a new ward.

The ceremony's similar all over the world – a white ribbon stretched across the main entrance, the medical staff and all the patients who can walk standing on either side with local dignitaries. A few speeches later I was handed the scissors to cut the ribbon. I tried, but unfortunately the scissors wouldn't cut. I tried again. The ribbon just got caught between the blades. I say blades. That was the trouble. The scissors were real silver, made especially by the local silversmith in the bazaar but they were too blunt to cut.

Then smiles of embarrassment gave way to relief as a resourceful nurse passed over a pair of surgical scissors, stainless steel and sharp. They worked. We all laughed and forgot about it. Weeks later, when I was back home, a parcel arrived. Inside was the silver bowl with a letter. They'd taken the original scissors back to the silversmith and he'd reused the silver to make the bowl.

The scissors, blunt and not very useful, were given a second chance, and something beautiful had come out of it. It's always good to give people a second chance when things don't work out quite right. After all, we all need one.

Lord, help me to see the best in everyone I meet today. And thank you that you do the same for me.

Set a guard over my mouth, O Lord; keep watch over the door of my lips.

A young couple were getting married and decided on a honeymoon in Sydney, Australia. They booked their air tickets on the Internet. They said later the flight didn't seem to be quite as long as they'd expected, even allowing for an unexpected stop and transfer to a smaller plane. And when they landed the airport seemed pretty small. They were in Sydney all right but it was the small town of Sydney in Nova Scotia, Canada. Out in the boondocks. Apologies to the folk who live there if it's an unfair description of the place, but it didn't have much night life.

I heard of a similar misunderstanding, more easily resolved, when a travel agent offered a self-catering apartment in Turkey to a couple who wanted to go to Torquay. Misunderstandings. What seems crystal clear to me may not be so to someone else. And maybe their misunderstanding of what I say may not be because they're complete idiots but simply that I didn't explain myself as clearly as I might have done. Or thought I had.

I can usually see very clearly in my head exactly what I want to say but the words don't always come out quite right. And that's true for all of us. We're only human, after all.

So the word today is think before we speak, give people the benefit of the doubt when they speak and, whether you're booking a holiday or working on a relationship, make sure you both know where you're going.

Incidentally I heard that the young couple had a great holiday anyway. That's love for you.

Lord, lead me in your ways and forgive me when I stray.

Praise the Lord, O my soul, and forget not all his benefits – who forgives all your sins and heals all your diseases, who redeems your life from the pit and crowns you with love and compassion...

An American gold prospector – yes, they still exist – was working in an isolated area in the Rockies when he was caught in a blizzard. He took shelter but the snow continued and piled up for a couple of days. Then, as he tried to get down the mountain, an avalanche buried him. Deeply.

Under the weight of several feet of snow he found he could just manage to move his arms but he didn't know which way was up. To dig the wrong way would have taken him deeper into the snow and he would have died. After the panic stopped, he worked out which way gravity was making his tears trickle around his eyes and on his cheeks. That was the clue he needed.

He began to dig. He struggled for what seemed like days and after exhausting, sometimes frantic, efforts his hands broke through to the surface and he was free. He still had a two-day journey down the mountain to safety, but he made it. Describing the experience, one thing he said caught my attention. "I've spent years searching for gold and never found any. But now I know what rich is."

And it had nothing to do with gold. After the avalanche, to be alive was riches. To see the sky, to breathe the air, to get home and see the people he loved, that was enough. That was riches. That was what gave value to his life and does to mine. Winning the lottery might be fine but most of us are rich without it.

Lord, I'm rich, your blessings overwhelm me. Teach me to share as you have shared with me.

Overleaf:
High Summer, Olympic Mountains, *Watercolour*

Humble yourselves, therefore, under God's mighty hand, that he may lift you up in due time. Cast all your anxiety on him because he cares for you.

It's a big wastepaper basket, one of the biggest I've seen. It sits there quietly in the middle of my studio. It looks hungry, its mouth open, waiting for me to feed it something. It tries to disguise itself by looking pretty. The outside's printed with pictures of Mickey Mouse and his partner Minnie. I've never quite worked out what their relationship really is, but I suppose that's their own business anyway.

Both Minnie and Mickey are smiling. I suspect the smile comes from watching me struggle over a painting or something I'm trying to write. The paper basket can fill up twice a week with drawings I've scrapped, or scribbled thoughts for the day that didn't work out. But in the end it's just paper and I try to recycle a lot of it anyway.

What I'd really like would be a waste bin I could throw my frustration in. And those impatient replies I give when I'm tired. Just to abandon them as so much rubbish, leave them there and forget about them. That'd be great.

I get particularly sad when I hear someone who's had a terrible experience say, "I can never forgive that." I know they've been deeply hurt, but longheld resentment hurts the holder more than the one it's aimed at. It sours life. So whenever you feel bad about someone or something, imagine a wastepaper basket as big as mine, throw it all in, dust off your hands and start again. It's worth the effort.

Lord of yesterday, I give you my frustrations and my fears. Take them, and let me start again, each day.

For God did not give us a spirit of timidity, but a spirit of power, of love and of self-discipline.

The birds are singing, the magnolia's come and gone and spring is here again – I can tell that by the weeds in our garden. Weeds are so enthusiastic. The flowers I plant out and nurture need loads of loving care, but not the weeds. They grow with no help from me. The minute we've weeded one patch of ground and moved on to the next, the weeds are back again. Legions of green advancing remorselessly. Sometimes when I'm feeling particularly paranoid I'm convinced I can hear them laughing.

It's a never-ending struggle. I've suggested turning the whole garden into a dandelion reserve or a butterfly sanctuary but my wife's not convinced. And I don't think the neighbours would be too impressed either. There are no short cuts to a good garden, you just have to keep on with it and eventually, hopefully, it blossoms into beauty.

It's the same with relationships, whether it's friendship or something deeper and more intimate. However loving, every relationship hits problems at times and the easy thing is to give up. No, I'll rephrase that. It's never easy to give up a relationship, but sometimes it's easier to give up than to go on trying. Easier to let the weeds grow. But like the garden we have to work at relationships. Weeding out the criticism, the rough words. Weeding's best done on our knees and the same goes for relationships. A little humility and a little prayer can go a long way.

Lord, when I'm tempted to give up and turn away, just let me see you on the road ahead of me.

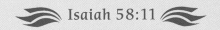
Isaiah 58:11

You will be like a well-watered garden, like a spring whose waters never fail.

It's amazing what a garden can tell you. When I take the dog for a walk I look at front gardens. So does the dog, although his motives are different, particularly when he sees trees. There's one road with bungalows. There are only two designs, so there's not much variety in the architecture, but the residents express themselves in their gardens.

Some gardens are very disciplined. Neat square lawns, each blade of grass hardly daring to move. In the beds, geraniums planted every 15 inches and blue lobelia in between. Then come the slightly weedy gardens, the plants not as carefully tended but enjoying their freedom a bit more. A few plots are almost totally paved over, or gravelled, with just a couple of rocks and a few shrubs – low maintenance. And there's always one with a high privet hedge to protect the owner's privacy. I'm glad to say there are no totally neglected ones.

I leave it to the amateur psychologists to decide what the gardens say about the gardeners. I'm not going to risk that in public although I have my own ideas, but the gardens that lift my spirits most are the ones that are a riot of colour. They may be a bit untidy with the occasional weed, but they're full of life and joy and beauty. They're the ones that appeal to me most and they're the people too who light up my life with colour.

Lord of all joy, give me the courage to step through the garden gate and live today with you.

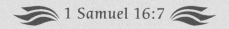

"The Lord does not look at the things man looks at. Man looks at the outward appearance, but the Lord looks at the heart."

I loved beachcombing as a child. I still do, given half a chance. It's the anticipation in walking up and down the tideline looking for treasure. Treasure can be a beautiful shell, a polished stone or a worn bit of driftwood. I've been fortunate. I've beachcombed on isolated islands in Indonesia, along the New Zealand coast, in southern India and many other places.

A shell found on the beach is always empty. There's no sign of the creature that made and lived in it, but what a work of art a shell is. The colour and symmetry of the spirals programmed into its creation. A wonder we take for granted. "Just another shell," we say. Looking at one the other day I noticed how different its textures were. The outside hard and rough, abraded by the constant movement of sand and waves, but the inside smooth to the touch, without blemish. And that's where its owner lived – inside.

Most of us have a fairly rough exterior although some hide it well. It's the shell we live in to protect our privacy and prevent people from prying into our lives. How hard our shell is depends on how life's treated us. For some it's become so hard it's difficult to penetrate, but inside we're all softer, more vulnerable. Don't be put off by the surface feel. Wait, and you may find a very different person inside. Someone to treasure.

Lord, let me look below the surface of life and find the treasure hidden deep inside.

Overleaf:
Chasing the Gulls, *Watercolour*

...so in Christ we who are many form one body, and each member belongs to all the others. We have different gifts, according to the grace given us.

I had another thought about seashells. I'd been walking on the South Downs, the rolling uplands of Sussex. All made of chalk I'm told. Not the little white sticks we used to throw at each other at school when the teacher wasn't looking, but the natural rock.

The Downs are made of billions of tiny seashells from creatures living long ago. When they died their shells sank down onto the seabed, layer upon layer. Over time the pressure hardened and compacted them into rock and then, in some great cataclysmic shift in the earth's surface, the layers of shells were raised out of the sea to become the Downs. Why they're called Downs when they were raised up I don't know, but we'll move on.

Few of us are called to be great but we're all called to be something. Few of us achieve fame but we each have something we can give to the community in which we live.

John Donne, a poet and preacher who lived 400 years ago said, "No man is an Island, entire of itself; every man is a piece of the Continent, a part of the main." In other words we're all part of humankind and, although we're each a pretty small part, without us the world would be poorer, and together we add up to something significant. Tell yourself today that you're valuable, your life is important and that you have something to give. Then go out and give it.

Help me to see the value of the folk I meet today, and thank you, Lord, for the price you set on me.

Accept one another, then, just as Christ accepted you...

Some people read the newspaper in the loo. That's easier with a tabloid than a broadsheet. But the other day a little book appeared on the window sill in there. It was called *The Little Book of Calm* and the great thing about the book is that each page holds just one thought, a couple of sentences that you can read quickly and take to heart.

I say 'take to heart' – some of them you can take with a pinch of salt, like the one that says, 'Wear comfortable shoes'. A good idea but not at the top of my list when it comes to measures to calm me down. 'Breathe less' is another. Slowing your breathing can help to calm you, but don't try to cut it out altogether. That would certainly calm you down but you wouldn't really feel the benefit.

Others are more helpful. 'Pretend to be human. Leave it to others to be perfect.' Now that's good advice. We try so hard to live up to other people's expectations, and our own. We try to be supermen and superwomen. Super cooks and super parents. We try to do everything perfectly. But it's not necessary. Now don't get me wrong. It's great to try to do the best we can but don't strive for the impossible. We're only human and that means none of us is perfect.

However hard we may try, we'll never be Nelson Mandela or Mother Teresa, Tom Cruise or Nicole Kidman. Just be happy to be you. Accept yourself as you are, that's the way Jesus accepts you, and then maybe a little calm will come into your life today.

Lord, you take my breath away. It's good to know that I'm accepted as I am. Teach me to open my arms to others as wide as yours are to me.

There is a time for everything, and a season for every activity under heaven.

We've just redecorated the kitchen. Barbara wanted something bright and sunny so she chose a warm yellow emulsion to lift the mood. It looked good and a bright yellow tablecloth completed it. But walking round a furniture store the other day we saw a wall clock. A clear design and the plastic surround was yellow. A good match for the walls and it was cheap. We bought it.

So what to do with the old clock? It was still working. "I know," I said, "I'll put it in my studio. There's no clock there and I've got a space on the wall it'll just fit." I found the hammer and a picture hook, grabbed the steps and then...I paused. "Why on earth do I need a clock in my studio?" I asked myself. That's where I paint and write my books. I don't want to look up for the time when I'm painting my next masterpiece. (That'll be the day!)

Some things can't be ruled by the clock. I'm all for punctuality when it's important. Getting to work on time, or not keeping friends waiting by turning up half an hour late. But we need moments – and longer than moments – when time takes second place and we allow ourselves to relax.

The poet T.S. Eliot wrote about 'the still point of the turning world'. A store from which the world gets its energy. A virtual place where we can drop the rushing around, where we can meet ourselves and be ourselves and renew our energy and inspiration. Some of us call that still point God.

Timeless Lord, I meet you most easily in the quiet of the day. Help me to find you in the crowded moments too.

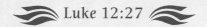 Luke 12:27

*"Consider how the lilies grow. They do not labour or spin.
Yet I tell you, not even Solomon in all his splendour
was dressed like one of these."*

A friend gave us an amaryllis bulb, complete with plastic pot and a small bag of compost. The bulb looked dry, lifeless, with a tangle of desiccated white roots but we potted it up, watered it, and put it on a warm window sill in the light.

Transformation. Three or four days later the first shoot appeared. It was very pale green and tentative, as though it was just sticking its head above the parapet to see what was going on, and ready to duck down again if it didn't like what it saw. Each day it grew a little bigger, stronger, a slightly darker green. Then a second leaf appeared.

That's where it is now but I know from past experience that in a few weeks there'll be a straight and robust stem, several long dark green leaves and then the final glory of those huge brilliant scarlet flowers singing silent praise to their creator. That's God, not me, I only watered it. Actually, I didn't do much of that either. Barbara did.

When we were given the bulb we could have kept it carefully wrapped up in its box but then it would never have grown. There'd have been no life, no flowers, no beauty. Life's for living. It can be tempting to stay quietly in our own little corner ignoring the world at large, but we can't, not really. We're part of the world, with all its ups and downs and we have a share in it. So come out of your box today, root yourself in reality and try life. There's a lot of beauty out there if you look for it. And you might even get in touch with the creator of it all.

*Lord of all energy, I come alive in you. Help me to share the joy
and thrill of living out your purposes.*

Overleaf:
Cottage by the Sea, Scotland, *Watercolour*

Dear children, let us not love with words or tongue but with actions and in truth.

I've just had a birthday. I'm not telling you which one. I'm too old to reveal it without good cause but not old enough to have lived so long that I'm proud to tell everyone I meet. So it's just a birthday. Birthdays remind me of an exchange in court between a lawyer and a witness. The lawyer asked, "What's your date of birth?" Answer: "28 May." "What year?" "Every year."

But it's the birthday cards I want to think about. Four of them came from the four grandchildren. They're all handmade – the cards, not the grandchildren. Handmade, drawn and painted. The cards range from a very exuberant abstract from Georgia, then aged 3, to a bright orange and black tiger in the jungle from Claudia, five. Then there's Jessamy's. She's ten and produced a detailed 'Artist at Work in his Studio' while her brother Sam, a sophisticated 12-year-old, has drawn a hard-edged cartoon.

The great thing is they've made them themselves. They've sat down, thought out what they were going to draw and then spent time creating it. That gives the cards a value far beyond the mass-produced and overpriced cards we find in the shops. Each of my cards was produced with loving care especially for me.

That's what makes relationships special too. However much or little money we have, we can give a little time and care to strengthen them. And that's what shows our love – the effort we're prepared to put into it.

Loving Lord, I live in you or not at all. Teach me to live and love through every breath I take today.

 Hebrews 12:1

...let us run with perseverance the race marked out for us.

Two boxes of pastels are sitting on a table in my studio. Pastels – the coloured chalks artists use. Not the gentle colours clothes designers describe when they say, "This year's colours will be pastel shades..." But a whole rainbow of brilliant hues. Bright yellows, orange, 12 shades of red from bright vermilion to deepest carmine, and on to violet. Then blues, greens and what we call earth colours – the natural ochres and browns. Exciting, to an artist anyway.

And there they sit in their boxes, looking beautiful. Seems a shame to disturb them but I've got to take a deep breath, strip off the paper wrappings and begin to paint a picture with them. That's when it gets really interesting, although it's never quite as easy as you think it will be. I've known amateur artists who try pastels, find the first results disappointing and give them up. The pastels finish up in the dark recesses of a cupboard. Incidentally the word 'amateur' isn't a criticism – it's from the Latin word for love, so an amateur's someone who does it for the love of it.

But I got busy with mine and after a couple of days those lovely pastels are all jumbled up. The paper wrappings in shreds, some of the pastels worn, others broken into smaller lengths. They've been used, and they've helped me create a couple of decent paintings.

New Year resolutions are great. All the things we commit ourselves to do, or not do, in the coming year. The trouble is it's harder to live them out than to think of them. It's not the New Year resolutions that count, it's the resolution with which we paint the picture, live it out.

Thank you, Lord, for the gifts you give. Help me to use them for others – and for you.

Overleaf:
Morning Glory, *Watercolour*

List of references in biblical order

TLM International
80 Windmill Road
Brentford
Middlesex TW8 0QH
United Kingdom
Tel: 020 8326 6767
Fax: 020 8326 6777
friends@tlmint.org
www.leprosymission.org

TLM Trading Limited
PO Box 212
Peterborough PE2 5GD
United Kingdom
Tel: 0845 1662253
Fax: 01733 239258
enquiries@tlmtrading.com
www.tlmtrading.com

TLM Africa Regional Office
PO Box 11104
Hatfield
0028 Pretoria
South Africa
Tel: 00 27 12 8035529
Fax: 00 27 12 8035529

TLM Australia
PO Box 293
Box Hill
Victoria 3128
Tel: 61 39890 0577
Fax: 61 39890 0550
tlmaust@leprosymission
.org.au
www.leprosymission.org.au

TLM Belgium
PO Box 20
Vilvoorde 1800
Tel: 32 22519983
Fax: 32 22519983
leprazending@online.be

TLM Canada
75 The Donway West
Suite 1410
North York
Ontario M3C 2E9
Tel: 1 416 4413618
Fax: 1 416 4410203
tlm@tlmcanada.org
www.tlmcanada.org

TLM Denmark
Spedalskhedsmissionen
Peter Bangs Vej 1 D
DK - 2000 Frederiksberg
Tel: 45 3838 4888
Fax: 45 3887 1493
lepra@lepra.dk
www.lepra.dk

TLM England & Wales,
Channel Islands & Isle
of Man
Goldhay Way
Orton Goldhay
Peterborough PE2 5GZ
United Kingdom
Tel: 01733 370505
Fax: 01733 404880
post@tlmew.org.uk
www.leprosymission.org.uk

TLM Finland
Hakolahdentie
Helsinki 32A400200
Tel: 358 9 692 3690
Fax: 358 9 692 4323
eeva-liisa.moilanen
@kolumbus.fi

TLM France
18, rue Justin
92230 Gennevilliers
Tel: 33 1 4794 6776
pierregeiser@wanadoo.fr
www.leprosymission.org

TLM Germany
Küferstrasse 12
73728 Esslingen
Tel: 49 711 353 073
Fax: 49 711 350 8412
LEPRA-Mission@t-online.de
www.lepramission.de

TLM Hong Kong
GPO Box 380
Central Hong Kong
Tel: 85 228056362
Fax: 85 228056397

TLM Hungary
Alagi Ter 13
H-1151 Budapest
theofil@matavnet.hu

TLM India Regional Office
CNI Bhavan
16 Pandit Pant Marg
Delhi 110 001
Tel: 91 11 371 6920
Fax: 91 11 371 0803
reception@tlm-india.org

TLM Italy
Via Adda 13
I - 05100 Terni
Tel: 39 0744 811 218
agbertolino@librero.it

TLM Netherlands
Postbus 9027301
BD Apeldoorn
Tel: 31 55 3558535
Fax: 31 55 3554772
leprazending.nl@inter.nl.net

TLM New Zealand
P O Box 10-227
Auckland
Tel: 64 9 630 2818
Fax: 64 9 630 0784
david.hall@tlmnz.org.nz
www.leprosymission.org.nz

TLM Nigeria
1 Lad Kwali Road
off Paiko Road
PNMB 179, Minna
Niger State
Tel: 234 66 224 840
Fax: 234 66 223 433

TLM Northern Ireland
Leprosy House
44 Ulsterville Avenue
Belfast BT9 7AQ
Tel: 028 9038 1937
Fax: 028 9038 1842
colinferguson@tlm-ni.org
www.tlm-ni.org

TLM Norway
PO Box 2347
Solli
Arbingst. 11N 0201
Oslo
Tel: 47 2243 8110
Fax: 47 2243 8730
gaute.hetland
@bistandsnemnda.no

TLM Portugal
Casa Adelina
Sitio do Poio
8500 Portimao
Tel: 351 82 471180
Fax: 351 82 471516
coaa@mail.telepac.pt

TLM Republic of Ireland
5 St James Terrace
Clonskeagh Road
Dublin 6
Tel: 353 1269 8804
Fax: 353 1261 3757
leprosymissionl@eircom.net
www.leprosymission.ie

TLM Scotland
89 Barnton Street
Stirling FK8 1HJ
Tel: 01786 449 266
Fax: 01786 449 766
lindatodd@compuserve.com
www.biggar-net.co.uk/
/tlmscotland

TLM South East Asia
6001 Beach Road
#09-01 Golden Mile Tower
199589 Singapore
Tel: 65 6 294 0137
Fax: 65 6 294 7663
ditch@tlmsea.com.sg

TLM Southern Africa
PO Box 46002
Orange Grove 2119
South Africa
Tel: 27 11 440 6323
Fax: 27 11 440 6324
peter@tlm.co.za

TLM Spain
Apartado de Correos
51.332 CP
28080 Madrid
Tel: 34 91 594 5105
Fax: 34 91 594 5105
mundosolidari
@mx3.redestb.es

TLM Sweden
Magasinsgatan 4
SE-692
37 Kumla
Tel: 46 19 583790
Fax: 46 19 583741
info@lepramissionen.org

TLM Switzerland
Chemin de Réchoz 3
CH-1027 Lonay/Vaud
Tel: 41 21 8015081
Fax: 41 21 8031948
mecl@bluewin.ch
www.lepramission.ch

TLM USA
American Leprosy Missions
1 ALM Way
Greenville
S C 29601
Tel: 1 864 241 1750
Fax: 1 864 271 7062
psaunderson@leprosy.org

TLM Zimbabwe
PO Box BE 200
Belvedere
Harare
Tel: 263 4 741817
tlmzim@tlmzim.icon.co.zw